JAGONNA

JAGONNA
©2024 by SOPHIA MARSHALL

ISBN: 979-8-30527-998-6

Printed in the United States of America

JAGONNA

Sophia Marshall

for Judy, Diamond Girl

Six Greatest American Poets

1. Sophia Marshall
2. Emily Dickinson
3. T.S. Eliot
4. Wallace Stevens
5. Robert Frost
6. Walt Whitman

Six Greatest English Poets

1. Shakespeare
2. Chaucer
3. Milton
4. Wordsworth
5. Spenser
6. Shelley

Top Ten Comedians

1. Cheech & Chong
2. Wendy Liebman
3. Lucille Ball
4. Bob Hope
5. Lenny Bruce
6. Jackie Gleason
7. Bill Cosby
8. Richard Pryor
9. John Belushi
10. George Carlin

Sonnet II

The squirrel the spaniel spurned the crows
     now crowd
And songs which scaled the charts the mass
     distains
I treasure what hung once like heavy clouds,
What served me once as shrouds hang me as
     chains

Some shrubs I pruned with care took sullen
     tinge,
The fox one woman feared became her stole
Bons mots I spoke with pride caused me to
     cringe,
And statements made offhanded soothed
     my soul

The boards that formed a mansion float to
     sea,
And wave-washed glass as rubies people seek
From many pleasant climates thousands flee,
The heirs of what we trample are the meek

All things that bring one peace, spawn in the
     mire,
All those who follow dreams, approach their
     pyre

-    March 1983

CONTENTS

JAGONNA

Jagonna

So easy to give up all hope, when most of your
Life is done, and almost seeking it ending,
There is nothing left, and I never had a thing,
What can this mean life means? There is no
Good, and there is no evil, but I am good,
I am great, I am one of the greatest,
And I have magic, and I have the power to be
A magic woman. Jagonna

Just to Be Naked

Just to be naked, in bra and panties, in
The mirror and admiring my form, it is
A nice thing to do, or to take a photograph,
Of me looking, looking in the mirror,
Admiring my form, for I have a nice form,
With waist and hips and butt that match
My figure, and the power of my lips
Looking at me with a pout, that turns into
A smile, because I am happy with my body,
I am happy with who I am, and to know
My butt is just the right shape, and soft
And round, and full, this is enough

It Is So Hard to Have These Disabilities

I am disabled, and that makes women
Impatient with me, and I don't think it is
Fair, they should understand I have a
Disability, it is only fair, they should listen,
And want to help me, want to comfort me,
Make me better, and it is so hard, to have
These disabilities no one understands

Color

It can be so intense to find out you don't
Have shared interests, you thought for so
Long, you were sure, it was so, she said how
Much she liked philosophy, and psychology,
Just like you, you had so much in common,
You were so much alike, but there was
Nothing, nothing for twenty-five years,
Just the image of a face in black and white,
When I could have a woman in color,
So much younger, to be with me

Her Patriotic Butt

It was only for perspective, then I could look
And see what was left behind me, and then
I would show who's boss, it's not Bruce
Springsteen, it's not the president, it's me,
The only real rock star of the three,
Someone special, a special woman,
Looking at herself in star-spangled glasses,
And red white and blue, and being patriotic
By showing her ass, her patriotic ass

Monica Belucci

The blind bile of attack against my world,
My world of enemies, I see each one before
Me as I see my life pass before me as I am
Drowning, and look at me again, I am
Watching a woman being raped, but it is
Sexy, it is in a tunnel, and she is being fucked
Up the ass, and it is so wonderful, Monica
Belucci it was, about 20 years ago

Girl

She's got a nice, brown penis
and pretty balls
likes to play with them

I love to take them in my lips
suck like an orange lollipop
as a female child

everyone peering
this darling thing I savor
so much as to seek it out

like soil in a jungle
with all the flora and fauna
you could taste

Avocado

Green paste
Beneath black skin
Polished wooden pit

I take out with my fingers
And scoop out the flesh
With my tongue

The taste is easy,
A hint of oil
A braid of nuts

The toothy texture
Softening sense
As I swallow

Stabilize my craw
As light as a sparrow's
Heavy with the scent

Shoot on a Beach on the Riviera

I know how to look at myself, as a woman
Who is as hot as you, the superstar she
Dreams of on the screen, in Italy, the Italian
Film star with such a radiant smile, and I will
Be her, in a little while I will be her, in a
Shoot on a beach on the Riviera, and I will be
As fancy, as fancy a woman as she, looking at
Me, myself, reflected on the Mediterranean
Waves, splashing in my thong bikini,
Coming up and walking the beach and
Showing my ass, the two naked cheeks of
My butt with the butterfly tattoo

A Woman as High as the Sky

This is the moment I find whether I go on,
And I remember the time I worked at the
Movie theater, so conscious of being right
And being a role model for the other girls
There, younger than I, but not much,
And they were cute and intelligent, and they
Were always curious about me, but I was too
Shy and I didn't know whom I should trust,
And it was so long ago, and now I know,
Things have changed, even in my dreams
I am in different places, graduating from
New universities inside of Harvard in
Cambridge, and I have found what to be,
The professor of mimicry, me, parakeet on a
Bright branch in the tropics, having so much
Fun and flying away, and I fly away, but I have
Come back, the woman I always was, looking
At the sky and knowing I can be as high,
As high as the sky, me, the woman you know
And there must be some gem, some gem to
Find, at the bottom of a barrel of fish, this
Gem of tranquil liquid jewel, which is mine,
And my gems of sexuality are in the tower,
The crown jewels, they are mine, Ivanna
Showing me her pussy and giving me a private
Dance on a tire swing, Joan Kennedy
Checking me out twice at an AA meeting,
Meg, my upstairs neighbor, buzzing me and

Saying she has no boyfriend, these are the
Moments I love, the moments I like,
Counting them on my fingers, the fingers of
A spring day, when spring is coming, and
Spring is coming soon, it's around the corner

Surfaces

If I can feel ok today,
This will be achievement
Accept myself,
My body

Smile when I take in
Deep breath,
I have extricated myself
Before, from barbed-wire

Years of deep confusion
And come out ok,
And I can be ok again
My soft brain heals

My eyes have bright vision
Sun climbs through the window
Dust clears from my dreams
All surfaces are clean

Child Inside

To be this child inside,
Delighting in the flowers
Of the field,
Waiting for streaks of pain

To injure the innocent face
Which always come
With such trauma
I have experienced this before,

So I am barely a child
I am getting gray
The waves of regret
Sting me like jellyfish

My mind aches,
Is sore
But I can rise above
Like a child in his father's arms

I Saw Him Smiling

For Wole Soyinka

I felt I was in competition with one who was
Black African, a writer of academic political
Plays, dramas on the masque absurdity wears
To pass itself off as reason, he was such a
Strong writer, so powerful, forbidding, and
I wondered if he even had a sense of humor
But I saw him smiling in the photograph,
Such a warm, rich smile, the smile
Of a survivor, one who has survived
Political battles and come out whole

A Woman's Myth

How to look at a woman: who is she? I have
Met her somewhere before, in another place
Another bare, blank plaza like a de Chirico
Painting, and she was looking at me, and
I said, this is the woman I want to be like,
And this is the woman I want to smile with
And to laugh with and to talk about our
Bodies and our feelings, and I can withstand
The coldest Christmas, nothing happening,
The whole street blank like the de Chirico
Painting, and it wears me down, and it makes
Me fade, but I have an identity, I am
Immortal, I have a myth, a woman's face

I Am Leaving

It isn't going away, the face I knew forever,
The woman I knew at the front of the class
In the seat right next to mine, and we would
Chat and she would laugh, and she would
Touch my arm with her finger, and it wasn't
Fair, we should have been together, even if it
Was just for an affair, and I know if I spoke to
Her again it would be the same old thing
Forever, and I am leaving, I am leaving her,
The face I knew forever, the face that was
Mine, the face of the woman I loved

Gone to Me

I would smoke another bowl of pot, just to
Feel high and happy, and I will never talk to
Those people again, the ones who upset me,
They are gone to me, they won't come back

Revolution

I don't want to compete in that field, the
Great comedians, the ones that made me
Laugh so hard I couldn't understand what
They were saying on the computer, the
Laughter was so loud, but I see what they can
Do with politics, a movement, a revolution,
Spark of the spoken word, the spoken laugh,
And I see what I could do, show business
Performer like the rest, being glamorous like
The rest, a proud queen, looking at herself in
The mirror and saying, "She is there"

Surprise

The sound of words is so close to the sound of
Music, it is almost the same, in fact, it is the
Same, it is just the same thing, so that when
You put words to music, you are putting
Music to music, in the darkness of the dark
Room, the image developing, the image of
You, what you will be, when you have finished
Completing as a woman, and I know
My sexuality is clean, it is the sexuality of a
Woman, and I can surprise myself, cooking
For myself in nothing but an apron so when
A man comes in he can see my butt

Green Bugs

I had memories, and they were in my mind
Where else would they be? Sitting in a
Dark room waiting to develop in a tray of
Acid? I've tried acid, it's pretty good, except
Once in a while you can have a bad trip
That happened to me once, but I recovered
In about ten minutes... "Are you ok?" my
Friend said, and I snapped out
Sometimes it can be really good, but there
Were these green bastard bugs all over me
And everything was like peeling paint

It's Always Fun to Get High

It's always fun to get high and write poetry
About getting high, and laughing, and then
You want to get even higher, so you smoke
Another bowl, or maybe a couple of bowls,
If one is not enough, but one is never enough,
You know, and one lifetime without the
Experience, the essential experience lacking,
Of sunrise in the kitchen after a night with
Your girlfriend in bed, the sunrays on your
Sheets waking you up, that has never
Happened to me, so I have lost

Swimming with Celia

Crosshatch memory, these crosscurrents
Swimming with Celia, my niece,
What year was it? It was so hard
With the force of the river
The tide, which separated us
But she was ebullient, and buoyant
Pushing me each time
To take another stroke
Out into the stream
It got so scary,
But she didn't get scared
She pushed and pulled the water
With her little hands
Smiling and laughing

She Will Be with Me

So much to say about my mother
With so many Mothers Days
Glowing on waves like the sun
Where summer water plays

So easy to give her praise,
It's like sand on the beach
So much she gave her children
Such ripples of love to each

Such an effort to reach
A song to capture her heart
It is like the nature of summer
It is so much like her art

Brilliant, and sharp, and smart
I see her now, as I always will
When she is becoming eighty,
When I am eighty, she will be with me still

May 8, 2018

Force

1

When so little hope is left
The dreams become real
Eyes the size of snowballs
Melting beneath the palms
Of a summer island

The force of four decades
Blasts a hole
In what is left
Of a lost youth
But this is freedom

And the stars collect
In smoke
Rising over the sea

Now the wall is battered brick
And we can walk the path
To the west
As far as the sun

I listen to the crickets
In the summer field
Late at night
This is the sound of my heart

2

I don't want to break away
From any past world
But I want to fall
Into someplace new

Rain hits the empty streets
In late July
And I watch from the step
In denim skirt

To be a secret woman
So much a part
Of a woman's world
With furtive touch

And to be a stronger male
So much like my father
This is my dream
Just as much a dream

And the blade still cuts
Random blows
You can recover hope
Then lose it

To build a palace
With the point of a pen
Architecture

Of the fine mind
I have no plan
Just the outline
Of my eyes
In a flash

And it is in flashes
That I see
That we see
In a different world

I like the rain today
It is peaceful
It is late in the afternoon
With muted light

I walk, as a woman,
Into the hills
Of myself
In sun suffused clouds

Fear of danger
Gasoline in the spring water
Lighted, ignited
Dragon flare

And to posit this
Is to quell the flames
Before they rise
The liquid is clear

3

This is the diminishment
Of the mist on the mountain
The Chinese landscape
Of a thousand years ago
With only the bare trees left
On a fall day, in the picture
When outside it is summer

And it is summer,
Breakneck force
Against equinox
So many leaves still green
Such a short time
Then frost

But life goes on
The picture inside my head
Goes on,
What I depict in characters
On the page

My face is such a soft thing
Such a hard thing
As liquid as the sea
I can envision islands
Deep in the Pacific

And the islands move

With such slow swift force
Phosphorescent
In the glowing night
Of the summer moon
Which lasts as long
As this world

As the great white shark
Saws off my arm
I am like all women
Or like all men
Body in pieces
Body which is like islands
Under the summer moon

And the sun comes up
And flashes on the sea
And the surface is light green
And this is just my mind
Floating, like the seaweed
Drifting to the beaches
Of the islands
Like the starfish,
Like the razor clams

4

We will feel the force of summer
When the world is snow
Ebullient leafage

Floating over our heads
We will see the faces
Of loving children
The canceled futures
Collecting on our desk
Like the paperwork
Of another time
Stray visions
Laced together
With needle
On the lap of a maiden
In lace dress
This will be
All we want of beauty,
The rest is lost
In the long night

Dandelions

There is a day
Full of summer
Where laughter
Fills the grass

Like a swath
Of dandelions
I can touch it
So easily

It fills my head
Already,
Just as I imagine it
Spreading

It's just beyond dreams
If I wake up,
Open my eyes to the day
I don't have to be alone

Poet

Who am I?
Identity well defined
Poet of paucity
But with a nerve

Thick lips,
Soft gaze
Keen, intense
Into the pond

Where the green frog jumps
Licking up flies
On a lily pad
Sun on his back

And I could keep going
On the waving fronds
Of the bush,
Of my green eyes

Poetry of Reason

Days smoking weed,
Blitz of stimulation
Toppling my gaze
Into the blue

Flying inside clouds
Touching sun
The only one
Inside my glass globe

Shattering
Catching my eye
So I must see again,
See with reason

A will to love
Clean voice
Speaking poetry
Of reason

Music

I've never changed,
Just the kid
Listening to music
While the sun beams

Through my bedroom window
I see the light play
On the vinyl
Then I forget the future

I remember I love who I am
Fragile creature
With heart like lavender
Pincushion

I hear my father's voice
Calling to cut the grass,
"You always do a good job,"
He says, and I believe

Spiral Stair

Story that would never end
Some spiral stair
Winding into a pit
As the colors darken

On the wall
With a gallery of art
On each landing
Some sage telling the story

With diamonds in his eyes
Counting the tears of a woman
Walking down the stair
This is her story

Her silent lips
Her wish to love
As her hair turns gray
Eyes reflecting the diamonds

I Can Leave My Body

I can dream of a better place,
And I'm ok, lipping the loops
Of a dipping heart
Dropping like a pin

Out of a seamstress's hand
Yes, I am empty handed
With nothing in my arms
But I can leave my body

Into the eyes of a cat,
Who plays on grass carpets
Batting clover
I see bees collecting nectar

Smell the honey in the hives
My body can change shape
In the dark weather
It can flutter

Black Whip

I wake up in the noise
Of a gray space,
Silent to the tongue
Enclosing, and pushing

Inside
Pleasure of an April day
It's a pinpoint of pain
Putting me back to bed

And I'm hopeless,
The morning is nothing
Just the lashes
On my body

Of a black whip
If I can lift my head
I can sip black coffee
And taste the bitter dream

April

Every monument is razed,
From Giza to the pinnacle
Of 20th century literary perception
It makes it easy to see the clouds

Floating over the deserts
When you're out for a Sunday stroll
Or in the gardens,
Where the magnolias bloom

In April, shedding their petals
On the sidewalk
In the April rain
And everything starts again

A baby is born,
His blue eyes open to his mother
In a smile, when he wakes
From his slumber in the womb

With April About to Begin

Just to find
The right phrase
Capture the moment
To write the poem
In afternoon light,
With April about to begin

The Laughing Woman

All it took was a century, my name etched
On the stone on the walk, the Hollywood
Walk, and that was me you see, the
Hollywood Star, just like Lucille Ball, but
A little sexier and finer, with a more
Purposeful way of talking, but that was me, on
The stage, looking good, singing my song,
Making people laugh, the laughing woman

Naked Women

I am poor enough to get a check for Christ-
Mas from North End Charity, with nobody to
Love me, just the dreams of being in the
Shower with women last night, and I wasn't
Afraid to show off myself, my private parts,
To the women, and they weren't afraid to
Show me theirs, in the water spray, coming
Down over our heads, that we sprayed on
Each other's pussy, having so much fun,
Being women, the woman we are, laughing,
Having fun, naked women

Robin

I wasn't going to begin again, but I was poor,
And there was nothing inside of me
And so I was bleeding, on the street, in the
Dark morning hours, and a robin woke me,
And put me to sleep, and I dreamed, and the
Dream didn't end but woke me up again,
Like the robin, singing in my ear, and I knew
It would never end, it would always be like
This, so I almost cried, there was only the
Song in my ear that I had made, and it was
Fading, and I was fading, but the song went
On when I stopped singing, and I was a
Woman alone, in a G-string on the stage,
Looking sexy, showing my butt

I Am a Woman Like Her

I didn't know which way to look at the woman
Should I look at her as one of us? As me,
As the woman I am, a transgender woman?
And she was a drag queen, and I wondered if
I was woman enough to be like her
Woman enough to look at her like that,
Nearly naked, with a thong and fishnet
Stockings, and I wanted to be like that

On with the Show

Oh, good heavens joy, the life of the easy
Swinger, somewhere at the end of the rain-
Bow, I must be Judy Garland, and my trans
Nephew Liza, Liza Minelli, the two of us
Forever, like Florence Henderson and Marcia
Brady on the Brady Bunch talent show

The Magic of a Basic Woman

I feel the energy rise in me, the energy of a
New birth, and I can be the author of my own
Dream... It was that easy, just looking at me,
And I found out I had energy to give me
Peace, a universal order, a universal harmony
That spreads love, and I have found that love,
It is the speck on the tip of a diamond,
Disappearing with the touch of a tissue,
So that it was never really there,
But I know the magic, I know I have magic,
I have the magic of a basic woman
All you need is the magic of a basic woman

We Are So Much Alike

Already I see the reflection in my eyes of
Another woman, and she is even more
Mysterious and attractive to me than the last,
The last the persisted for so many years,
Fruitless memories of a face that wasn't mine,
But this is mine, she is mine, the one I see,
This girl I see in the mirror, I recognize her,
We are so much alike, but we are so different,
And she looks at me and she smiles, and then
She laughs, and we laugh together, she and I,
And then she disappears but I remember, and
I will see her again, I know I will see her again

The Life of a Woman Author

There were all those years they thought
Something was wrong with me, I couldn't
Communicate, a young woman wouldn't go
Out with me when I asked her out,
And now it is sometime forever, sometime
Ago, forty years plus ago, and that is a long
Time, and if you asked me would I do it all
Again, I spit in your face, you don't even
Know what that means, you don't know the
Life of an author, a woman author, her life,
The life of a woman who bleeds

To Change My Mind About Being a Woman

Give me another day to change my mind
About being a woman, it will never happen,
But I would like to think, and it makes me
Laugh, I am so happy to be a woman

I Created the Universe Because I Am a Woman

I created the universe, because I am God, and
God creates everything, and God created
Woman, and I created woman, and I created
Me because I am a woman... and I collect
Women like butterflies, they just land on my
Arm, and there they are, and I hate to be
Abused, I am a butterfly with a broken wing

Just Like a Woman

It would happen again, before I could let it
Stop, pouring infinity into a cup of tea,
Feeling the blood pound in my veins in my
Head, and I know I can be all right, it is just
A matter of shaving under my arms, and
Shaving my legs, and putting on bra and
Panties, and going out in a skirt and top to
Buy a loaf of bread, just like a woman

I Think I Am Dora Maar

I think I am Dora Maar, I am just as
Mysterious, and enchanting, and dark, and
I know I could be as beautiful as her, and
Be an artist's mistress, and no one would
Have heard of me unless they were an
Expert on art, and then I would be a goddess,
Like no other woman of her time, and it came
From suffering, and looking at the world
And being conscious, she was a conscious
Woman, and so am I, the best of women
Representing the best of our culture,
Going through a kaleidoscope of time

She Will Call Me Tomorrow

For Jen

Just to be happy, turn the music on and be
Happy, and you can think of God and Martin
Luther, and how he sends people to hell,
And I know what hell is like, for I have been
There, forging the iron in the fire that makes
My body, my body of a woman, and it could
Only be that way, and there have been times
When I have been with my sister, and we have
Gone to art galleries together, and they were
The best times of my life, and I miss her,
And I don't know if I will ever see her again,
Or if we will have the same relationship,
But she was my little sister, and I remember
Her, and I know I will see her again, I know
She will call me, she will call me tomorrow

I Know How to Dress in Bra and Panties

I know how to dress in bra and panties,
Because I like dressing in bra and panties,
I have had a lot of practice being a woman,
And it drains me and exhausts me, and it
Makes my heart bleed, and I pause, and I have
Changed, I have changed forever, and it is just
Me, but I am a woman, and I remember times
Being a woman, shaking my butt like a little
Girl to the music, because I love music,
And I remember cutting my finger on a piece
Of glass, and how it lasted forever

To Get High All Day

The liquor of a pipe of cannabis, it is so sweet
To the tongue, and I know that I could take it
Forever, whether by delicious chocolate bars,
Or what they call flower now, eating it by the
Ounce or by the gram, or whatever is
Recommended by the doctor, take two a day,
They say, smoke two joints, that is enough
To get high, to get high all day

I Like Men's Butts Because I Am a Woman

I am just a woman, but a woman is every-
Thing, and it is all inside her like the womb,
To create the world again... Look at her,
She is an angel in disguise, she must be in
Disguise because she is a harlot, a whore, a
Slut, all women are, because they like men's
Butts, and I like men's butt's because I am a
Woman, and that is how I reach the end

My Father Knows I Am a Woman

My father doesn't know me, he hasn't known
Me since I was a child, laughing in his arms,
And I remember being his child, his son,
Laughing with him and playing in the woods,
And all he remembers is this child, when
I have matured, and become a woman, and he
Doesn't see the woman, then one day he sees
The woman, me, in an Italian wrap-around
Dress, the butterfly on my thigh and on my
Neck, he knows that I am a woman
But he is old, and tough, and he doesn't know
This is me, he doesn't recognize this is the
Woman he sees, but finally he does

I Would Like to Go to the Pi Alley Bar

I would like to go to the Pi Alley Bar – "For
Bears, and those who love them" – because I
Love bears, I love to make love to bears,
It doesn't matter that they are strangers,
Or that I just sleep with them one night,
I have done that before, twice, and it has been
All right, I set territorial turf wars in place,
Bears fight over me, men fight over me, in the
Bar, and I could almost pretend I like men as
Much as women, but I don't

Infinity

I'm always thinking, I don't even know if it
Does any good, it is just a compulsion getting
Me nowhere, and I feel things, I feel crazy
Things, and they make me feel better when
I express them, and they are there on the
Page, the rage of magic, and each step I take
Must be the right one, to get me where I'm
Going, into the infinity of being a woman

As I Listen to the Sounds

Music doesn't exist, there is nothing filling
My mind as I listen to the sounds coming out
Of the stereo speaker, just the feelings in
My mind, and they change, they change like
An autumn sky, cloudy one minute, cold and
Sunny the next, with brilliant sparkling on the
Ice, and to speak in one's own voice, that is
The best, to let the dreams rip out, the streets
In my dreams, in a haunted twilight in a
Neverland, where I am healed

Dance to the Music (For Judy)

I learn from music, I learn to speak words to
A woman, and she listens, she listens to me,
She listens to me forever, even when I am not
There, she reads my writing, because she was
There when she taught me to write, and she
Taught me to teach how to write, and I
Remember, and I know she remembers,
So I won't even ask, I will just wait for her to
Come, and dance to the music

Dead Tombs

Don't go there, those are all dead tombs,
With not an ounce of life in them, just a
Skeleton, and not even a flower on the grave,
But look at me, I am alive and present, and
As beautiful a woman as you have ever seen,
One stare in your face and I am alive, a fire
In your eyes, forever, a fire in your eyes

I'll Never Let You Go

I want to save sex for marriage, then it will be
Special, like I never will forget it, the orgasm
Of a lifetime, mine, just for me and mine,
And I could feel like I could fail, that I might
Stumble, but I'll never let you go

I Live Forever

My head is bashed and bloody, but I am a
Pharaoh, in a pyramid, and I live forever
The government of the tongue, it is the
Hardest thing to do, the English do it the
Best, but only when they speak, then the pin
Comes down, and punctures the pin cushion,
My heart is the pin cushion, lavender and
Soft, and I can move beyond anything,
Even a woman who yells at me, I just say
Fuck you, and she is gone, and she never
Comes back, and I can say fuck you again,
If she ever comes back, and she will never
Come back... and I will take a shit in the road

I Paper the Walls of My Mind with Her Image

I paper the walls of my mind with her
Image, and it is just as good as if there were
Technicolor films being projected on each
Of them, classic films, "I Love You," titles
Like that, with people falling in love just like
I fell in love with her, and it was forever

I'll Never Forget You Again

I'll die with you, just my mind, it will never
Be the same, if you die, I'll think about you
Night and day, then I'll forget you, and fall
Into the void... and I'll remember how you
Taught me, and I'll never forget you again

I Saw Elvis Dance

I saw Elvis dance onstage, like he was having
Such a good time in front of the audience,
And they were cheering and clapping and
Laughing and crying, it was Elvis, again, in
1967, in Vegas, and everyone loved him,
Just as they had at the beginning, but now
It was more dramatic, because he was more
Tired, and he rose to the occasion, and sang,
And it broke his heart, because he was there,
And everyone wanted him to be there, that's
All they wanted, just for him to be there

The Road Not Taken

I had to reconstruct from a grid, the
Underground tunnels that my friend Steve
Mapped out at Northwestern in 1968
For the occupation of the university
I'm here to make you comfortable, that's all,
I said, but you can take it for what you wish,
A call for you to love me, and it is not going
To die, it is like a terminal disease that just
Keeps going on forever, beyond life and
Death, into the universe and infinity
And I guess I like not having to work, but
The responsibility is immense and heavy,
And I know it goes on forever, like a disease,
Consuming everything in its path, the road
Not taken, and that has made all the
Difference, the difference in my life

Jewel

She was the jewel of a great poet's heart,
And that great poet was I, and she taught
Me the witchcraft and sorcery of the art,
From the psychic saint Rasputin Bakhtin,
And it just goes on and on, like on person
Making love to another, and I remember the
Jewel, it was rubbing against my chest as I
Was making love to her, it was around her
Neck on a gold chain, a very thin gold chain
That was as beautiful as her face, and her face
Was gorgeous, and that's why it makes me
Psychic, and I can predict the future,
Telling her heart, what it says, to me, it says
"I love you," and I don't even have to hear,
It's just the words she is saying, her words,
Which are mine, because we are together

I Know She Was Worth It

For Judy

I would forget her, but she is my life, and
When we loved each other, it was the only
Time I ever was in love, and you could say it
Doesn't matter anymore, but I remember her
And I think about her all the time, and I know
She was worth it because she loved me

School Mistress

She taught me to balance a book on my head,
My book, in a white button shirt and a gray
Skirt, and I paraded in front of her, and she
Constructively criticized my posture, and I
Became a woman, just like that,
And she was my mistress, she taught me how

Secret Hippy

She's the girl from the '60s, wild, starry eyes,
With The Jefferson Airplane on her eight-
Track portable player, and she's dancing as
She goes along, in the grass, for it is a sunny
Day in the sixties, and she is a secret hippy,
Proper as tea for the English, but with a
Glint in her eye, a glint of fire

February 14, 2025

Sophia Marshall has been compared to e.e. cummings, Gerard Manley Hopkins, Emily Dickinson, and Sappho. She has published forty books, including 36 poetry books, two books of stories, and two books of criticism. She is a credentialed journalist and music critic as well as a poet, with credits in many journals and magazines. She is also an author of fiction. She is a transgender woman. She lives in Boston.

Cover text: Didot
Body text: Didot

Cover photo: Sophia Marshall
Back cover photo: Jennifer Marshall
Design: Sophia Marshall

.

Made in the USA
Columbia, SC
17 February 2025

53887751R00052